The Learning Works

*Editing and Typography by
Clark Editorial & Design*

Copyright © 1998
The Learning Works, Inc.
Santa Barbara, California 93160

The purchase of this book entitles the individual classroom teacher to reproduce copies for use in the classroom. The reproduction of any part for an entire school or school system or for commercial use is strictly prohibited.

Library of Congress Catalog Number:
98-067857

**ISBN 0-88160-322-8
LW 385**

Printed in the United States of America.

Introduction

Jewish Superdoodles contains step-by-step patterns for drawing pictures of items relating to Jewish people, holidays, and rituals. You can use these drawings to illustrate original stories, to make bookmarks or holiday greeting cards, or to create murals and stationery.

As you follow the steps on separate art paper, draw in pencil. Dotted lines appear in some steps. Make these lines light so that they can be easily erased later. Finish your drawing by going over it with colored pencils, crayons, or felt-tipped pens.

Each pattern is accompanied by an interesting fact or fun activity. *Jewish Superdoodles* is ideal for religious school projects, for rainy days, for travel, or for fun any time or any place!

Special thanks to Rabbi Rick Shapiro and Cantor Mark Childs of Congregation B'nai B'rith, Santa Barbara, California for their expertise and advice.

baby Moses

The Pharaoh's daughter found Moses in a basket when she went to the river to wash. Draw a picture of her finding Moses, and add tall reeds by the river bank.

JEWISH SUPERDOODLES
© The Learning Works, Inc.

3

challah

Challah is a braided bread that is eaten on Shabbat and other holidays. It is covered with a beautiful cloth. Decorate the cloth covering the challah.

Daniel

Daniel was thrown into a den of lions because he was found praying to God against the king's orders. Daniel was unharmed because of his faith. Draw Daniel in a den with three lions.

David

David was a young shepherd who loved to play the harp. He fought a giant named Goliath. Draw David with a sling in one hand and a rock in the other ready to fight Goliath.

JEWISH SUPERDOODLES
© The Learning Works, Inc.

6

dove

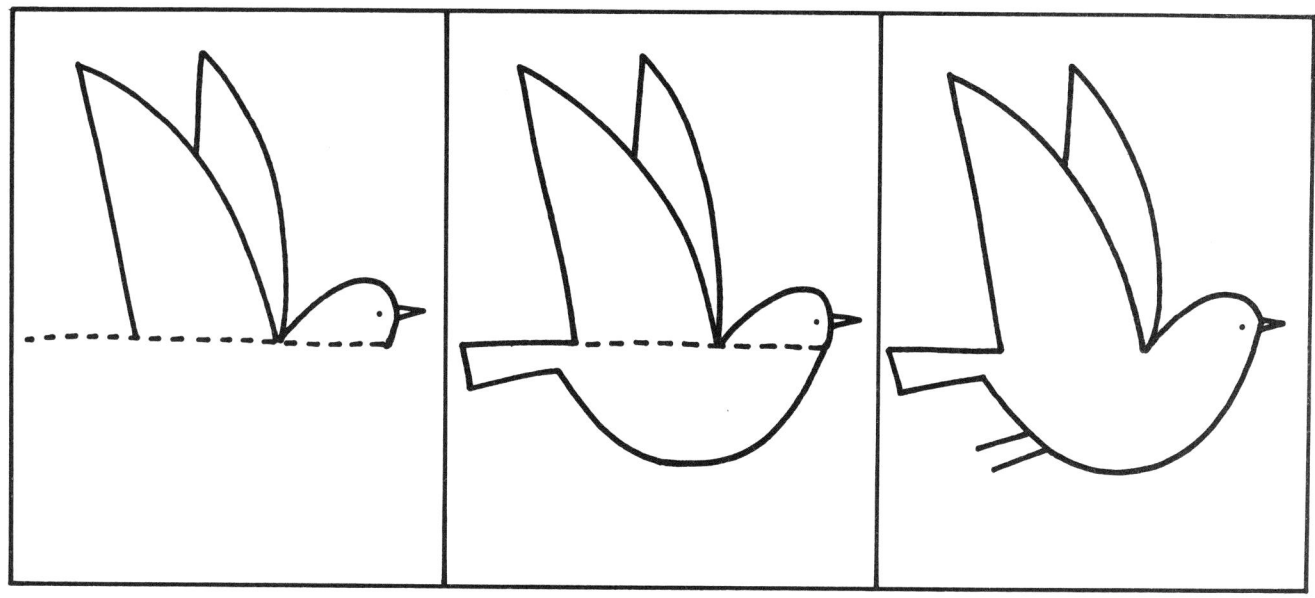

A dove brought Noah a branch to show him that the flood of forty days and nights was over. Draw an olive branch in the dove's beak.

JEWISH SUPERDOODLES
© The Learning Works, Inc.

dreidel

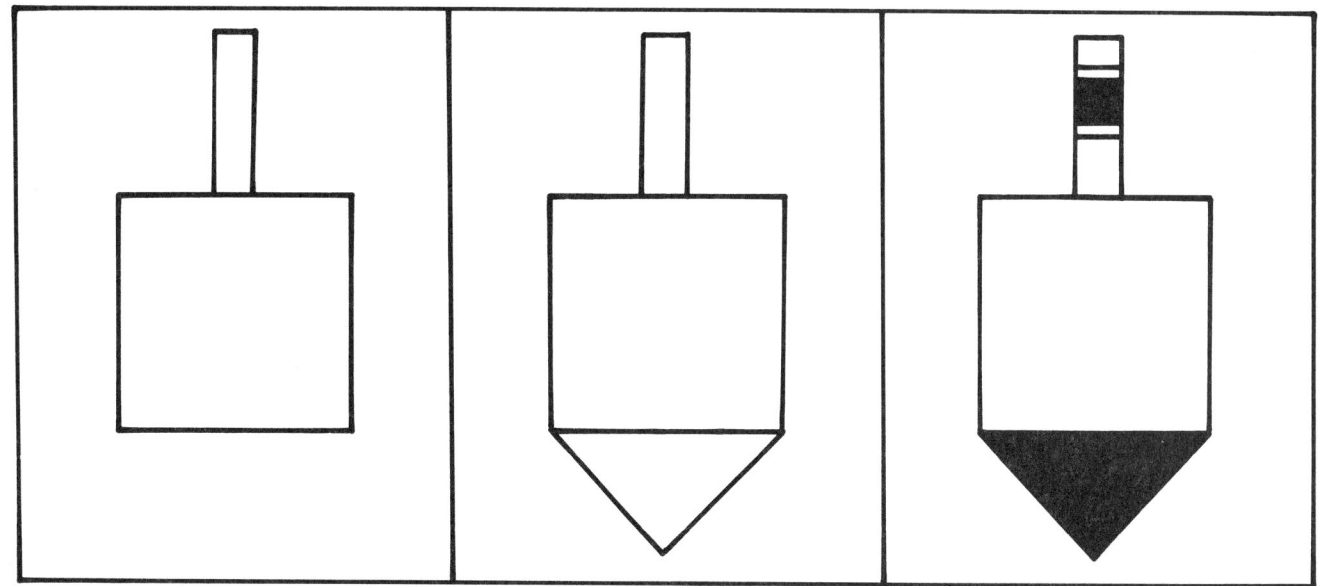

A dreidel is a four-sided spinning top. Kids play dreidel during Hanukkah. A dreidel has a Hebrew letter on each side: *nun, gimel, hey,* and *shin.* Draw one of these letters on your dreidel. ש ה ג נ

JEWISH SUPERDOODLES
© The Learning Works, Inc.

Eternal Light

The Eternal Light is also called the *Ner Tamid*. The light hangs above the Ark in the synagogue and burns continuously. Design and color an Ark. Add an Eternal Light and draw the burning flame.

flag of Israel

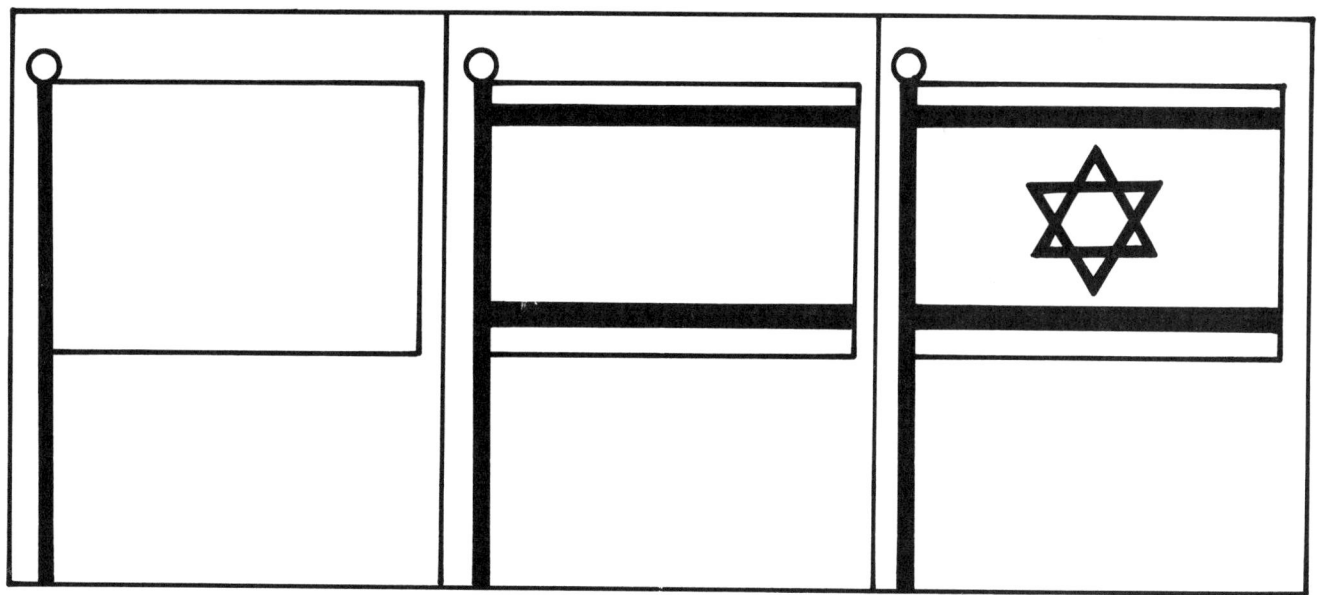

Israel became a nation in 1948. The two stripes on the flag are blue. Draw a person waving the flag of Israel.

JEWISH SUPERDOODLES
© The Learning Works, Inc.

Goliath

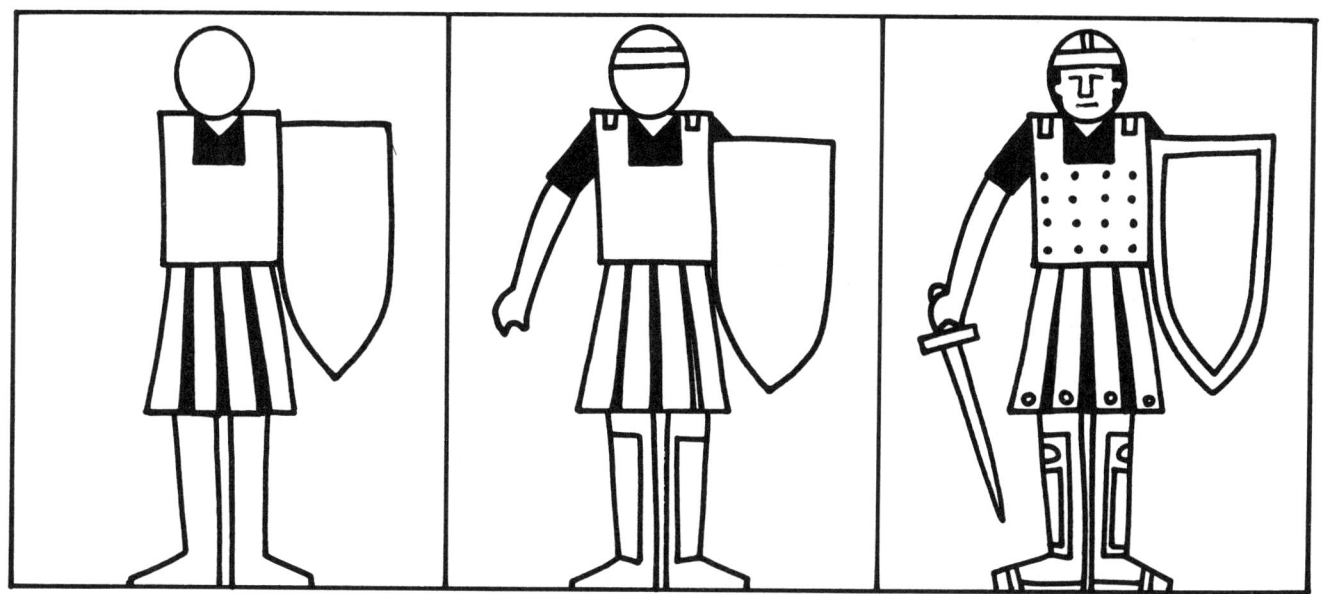

Goliath was a Philistine soldier who was nine feet tall. His armor weighed over 125 pounds. Draw a person who is six feet tall standing next to Goliath.

grogger

When the Megillah is read at Purim, everyone shakes noisemakers called groggers when the name Haman is mentioned. Draw someone in a Purim costume who is shaking a grogger.

Jonah and the whale

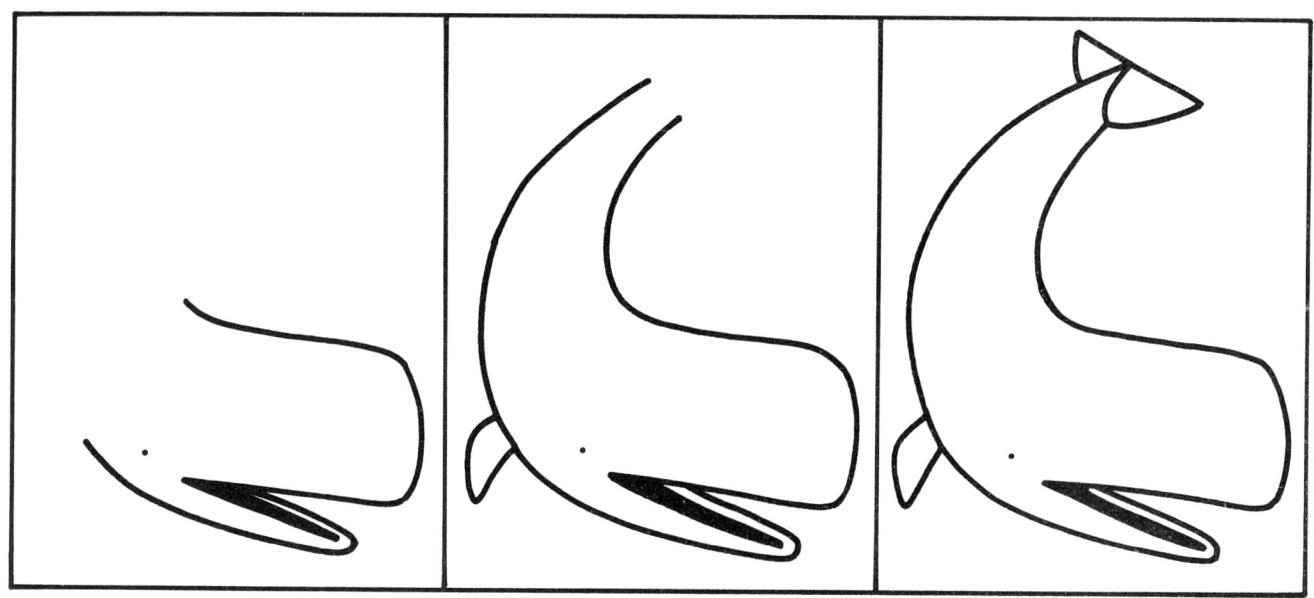

Jonah was swallowed by a huge fish, perhaps a whale, because he didn't obey God. After having time to think inside the fish's stomach, he decided to obey. The fish spit him up. Draw Jonah swimming away after leaving the fish's stomach.

Joseph's coat

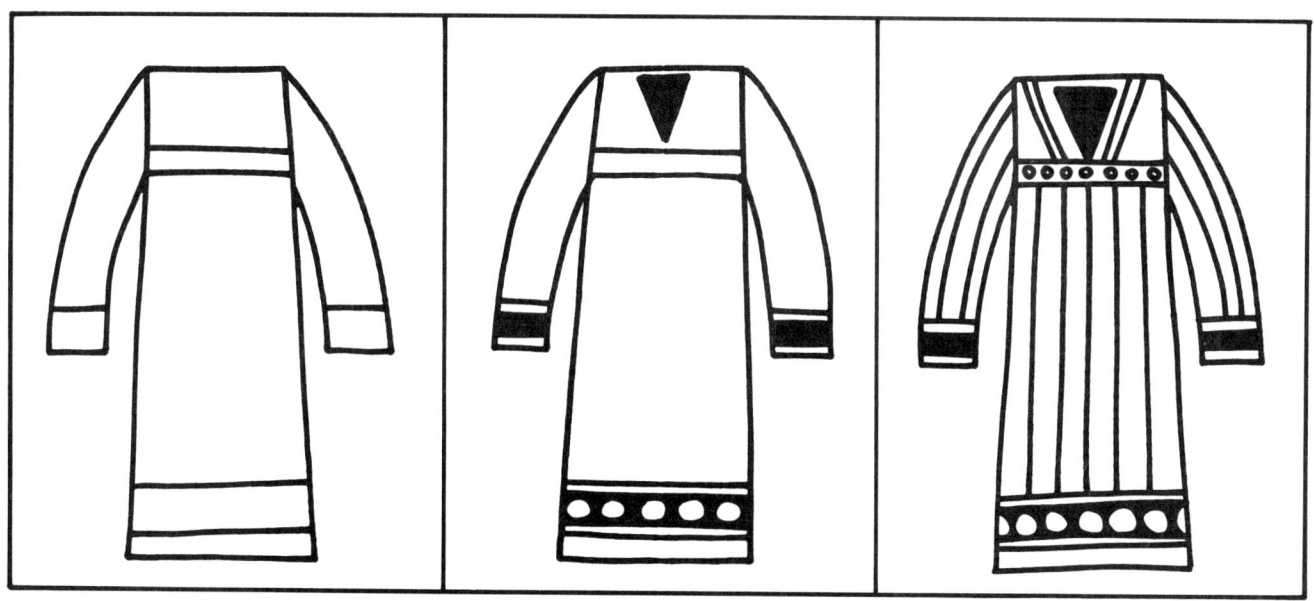

Joseph's father, Jacob, made him a coat of many colors. Joseph's eleven brothers were jealous of Joseph and sold him to Ishmaelites who took him to Egypt. Color Joseph's coat.

JEWISH SUPERDOODLES
© The Learning Works, Inc.

Kiddush cup

The Kiddush is a blessing recited over the wine to welcome the Sabbath and other holidays. Design a special Kiddush cup for your family.

kippah and tallit

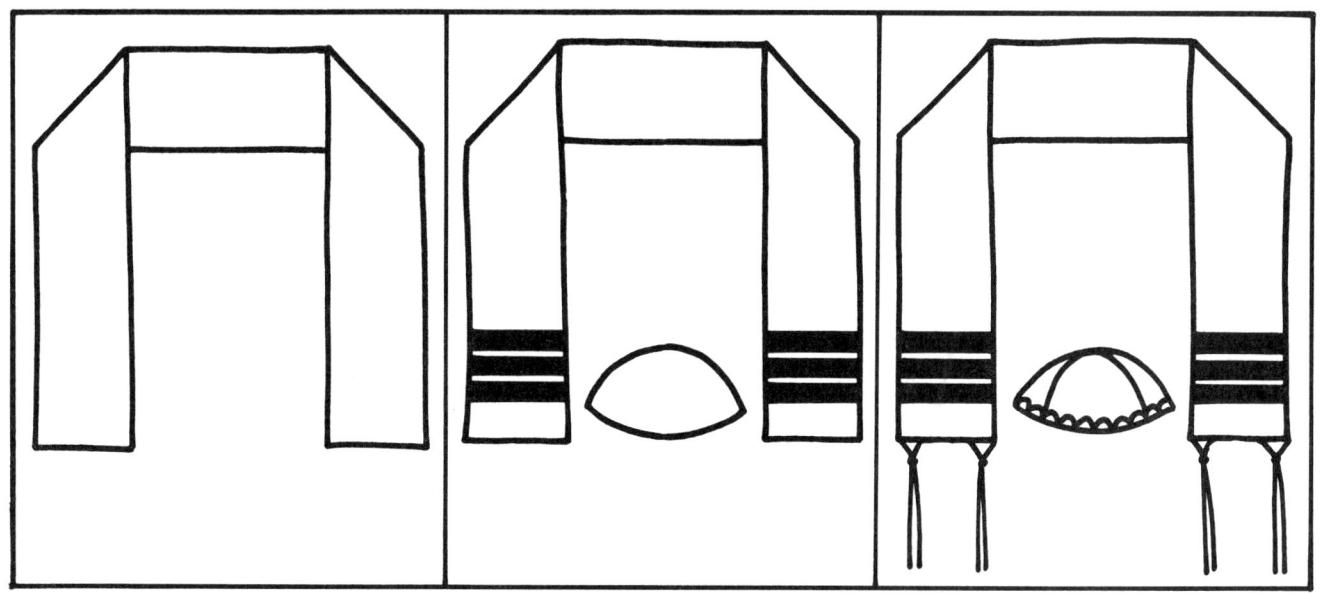

A kippah is a skullcap worn on the head. A tallit is a prayer shawl worn over the shoulders. The tallit has four corners and fringes called *tzitzit*. Draw a man wearing a kippah and a tallit.

lion of Judah

The lion of Judah is a symbol that appears on Torah covers, above the Ark, on menorahs, and on other Jewish items. Make a greeting card for a family member or a friend and use the lion of Judah in your design.

Maccabee

Maccabees were Hebrew soldiers who fought against the Assyrians. Draw Judah and four other Maccabees with their shields.

mantle and keter

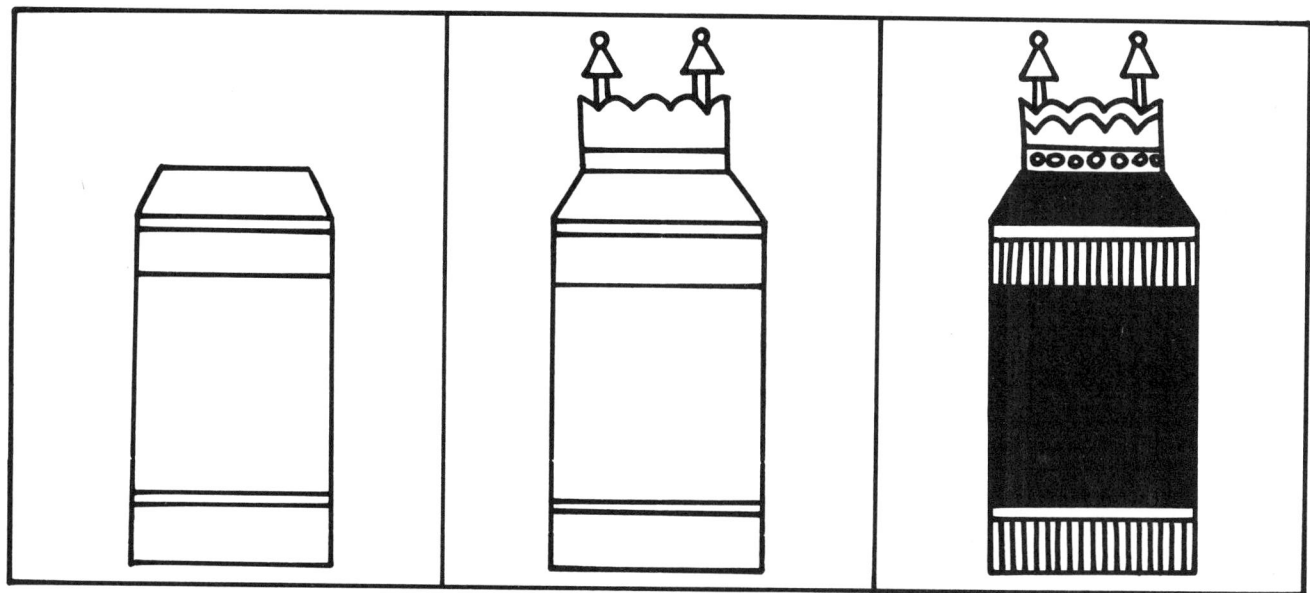

The cloth that covers the Torah is called a mantle. The keter is a crown that is usually made of silver. It goes over the top of the scroll. Draw and decorate a beautiful mantle and keter to cover the Torah.

menorah

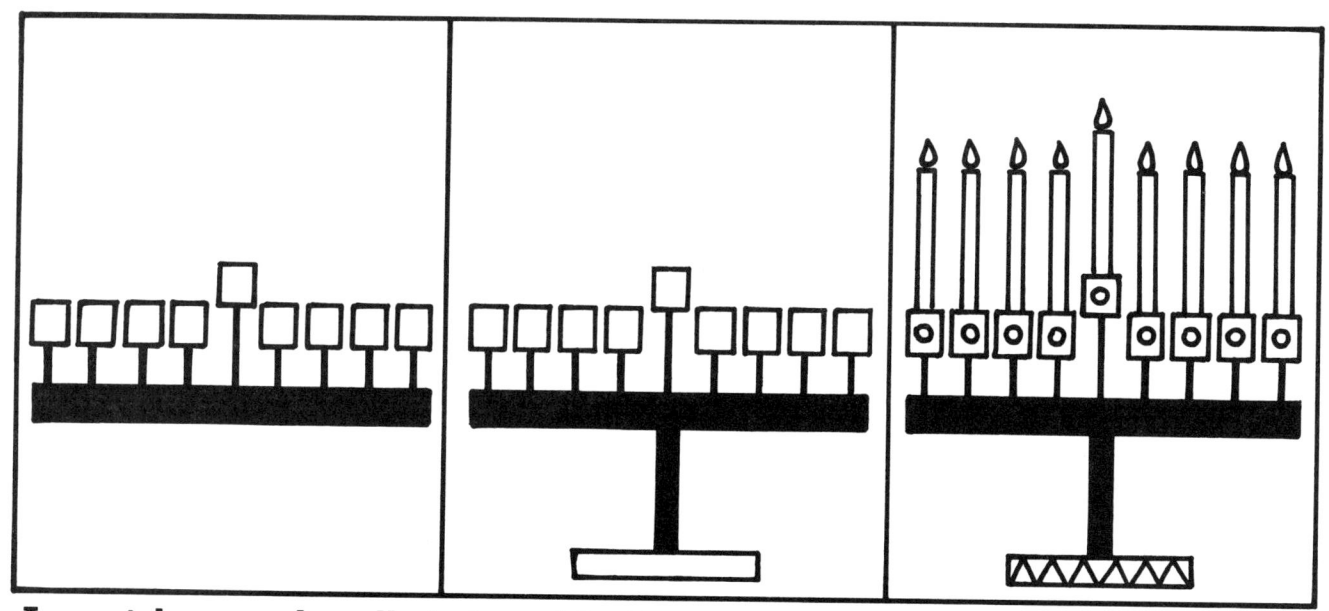

A special menorah, called a hanukkiah, is used during Hanukkah. It holds eight candles and the shamash, the helper candle. Draw your own hanukkiah.

mezuzah

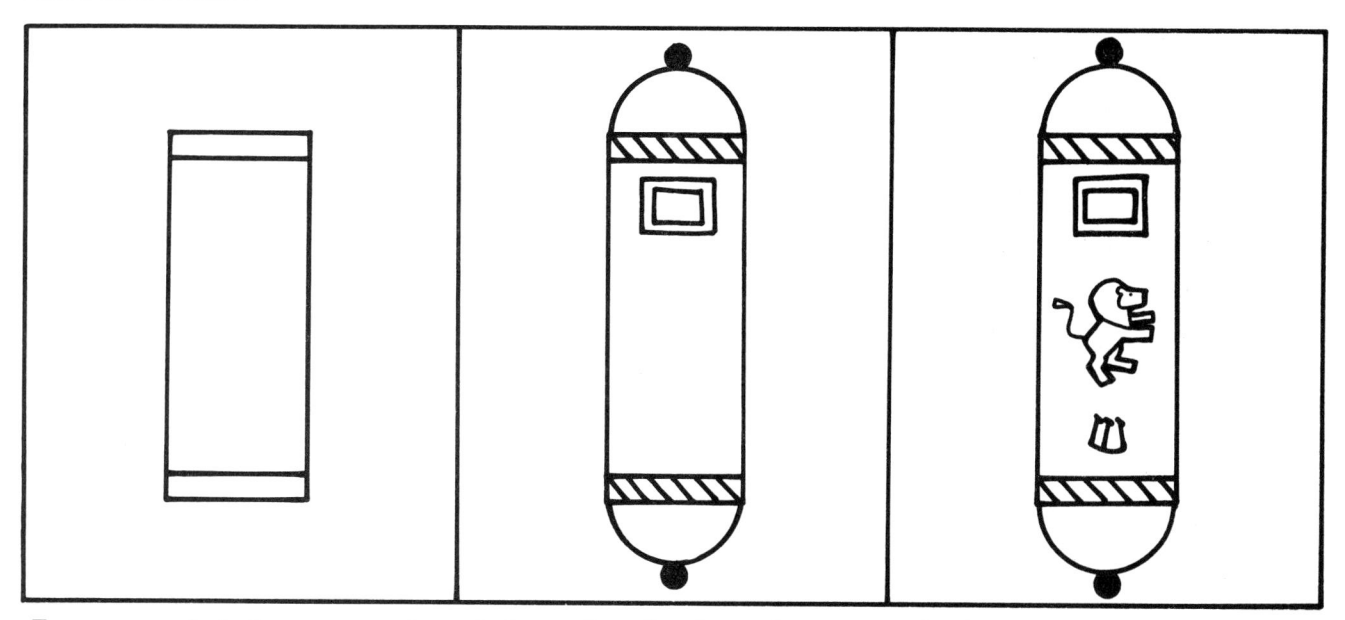

A mezuzah is hung on the right side of a door frame with the top slanted towards the inside of the house or room. Inside is a scroll with two passages from Deuteronomy. Create an original design for a mezuzah.

Noah's ark

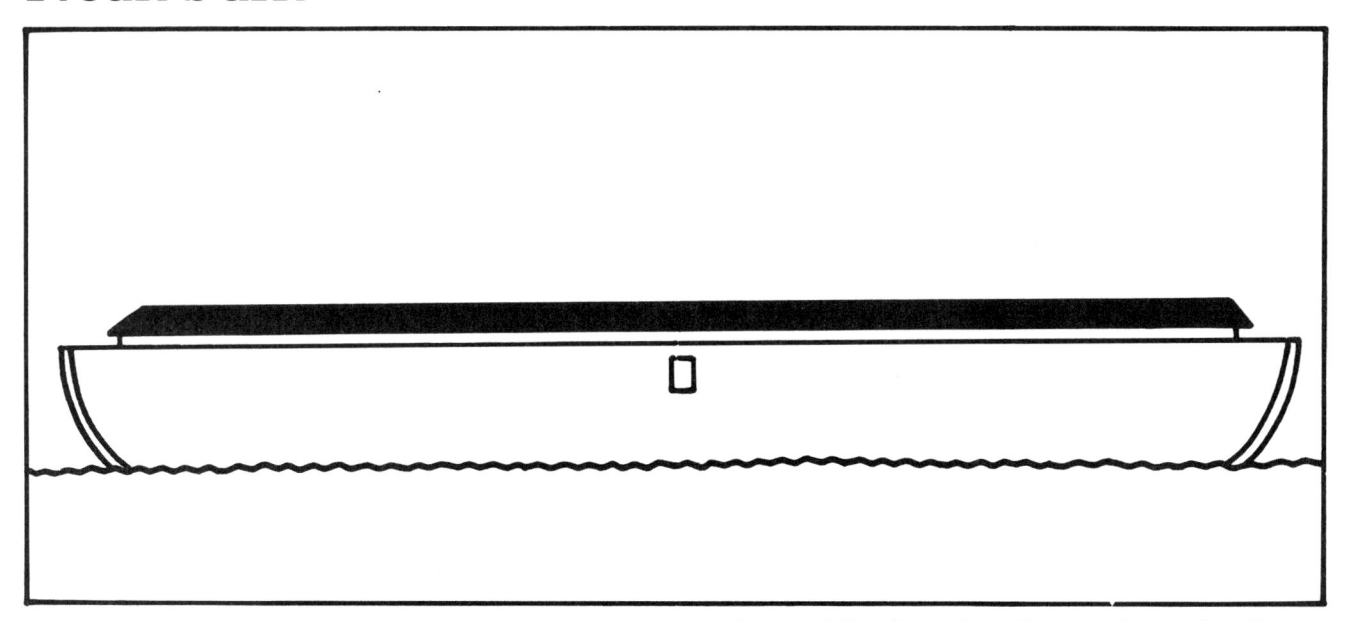

Noah's ark was almost twice as long as a jumbo jet! In the sky above the ark, draw a huge storm with clouds, rain, and lightning.

Noah's animals

Draw a line of animals in pairs waiting to board Noah's ark.

Noah's animals

Draw a line of animals in pairs waiting to board Noah's ark.

JEWISH SUPERDOODLES
© The Learning Works, Inc.

24

Queen Esther

Queen Esther helped save the lives of Persian Jews. Today Persia is called Iran. Design a crown for Queen Esther to wear.

JEWISH SUPERDOODLES
© The Learning Works, Inc.

seder plate

Design your own seder plate. Draw a roasted lamb bone *(zeroa)*, horseradish *(maror)*, a roasted egg *(betzah)*, a mixture of nuts, apples, and wine *(haroset)*, and some green vegetables *(karpas)* on your plate.

Shabbat candles

Candles are lit on Friday evenings at sunset to welcome the Sabbath. Draw a picture of a woman blessing the Shabbat candles. Draw her family around her.

shofar

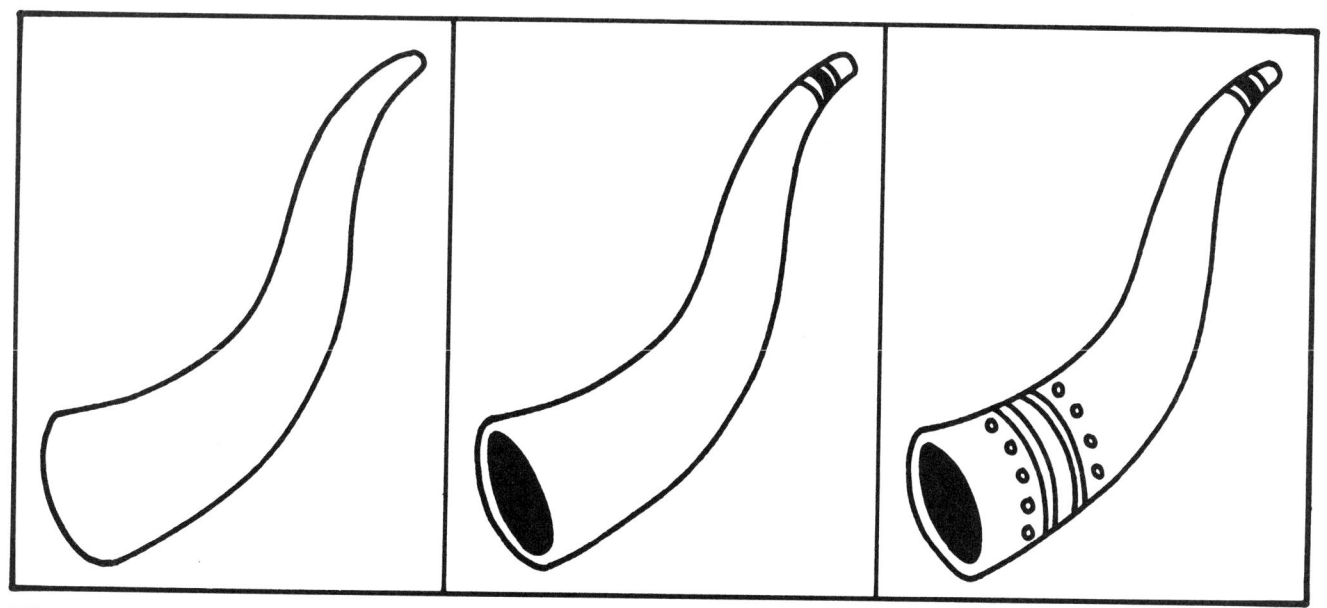

The shofar is made from the horn of a ram, a male sheep. Draw a picture of someone blowing the shofar at Rosh Hashanah and welcoming in the new year.

JEWISH SUPERDOODLES
© The Learning Works, Inc.

spice box

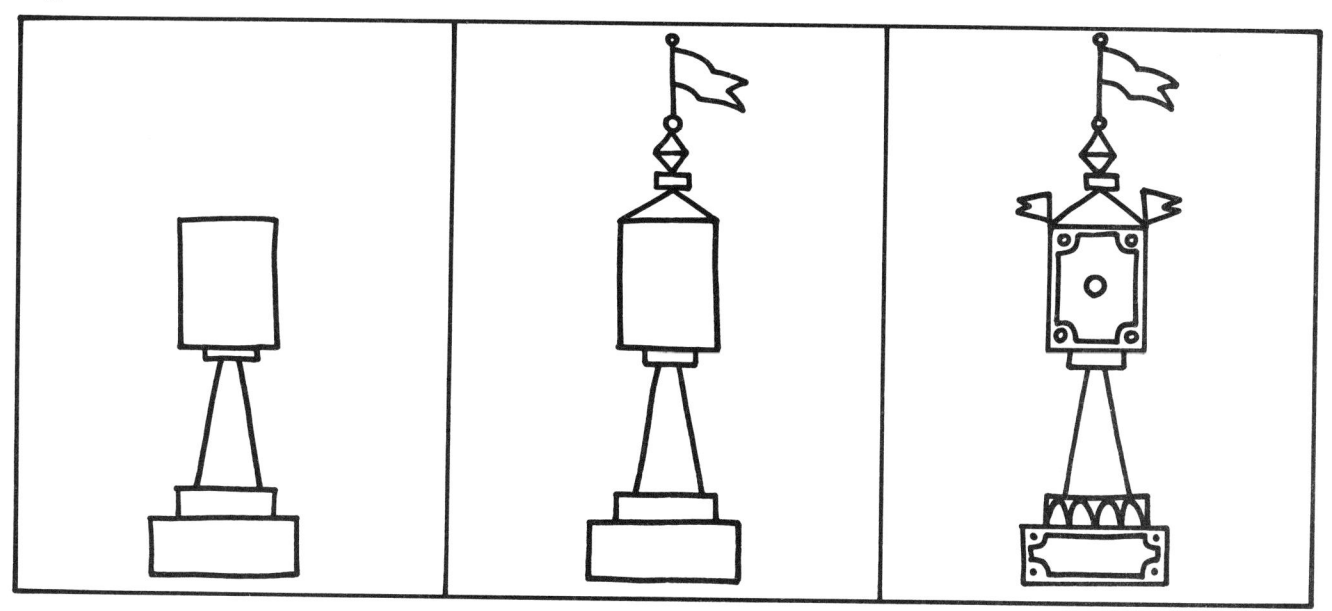

A spice box is used during the Havdalah service on Shabbat. Inside are sweet-smelling spices such as cloves and cinnamon. Draw someone holding a silver spice box on Shabbat.

sukkah

The sukkah is a hut built during Sukkot to celebrate the harvest. Its roof is covered with palm fronds. Draw fruit hanging from the roof and sides of your sukkah.

JEWISH SUPERDOODLES
© The Learning Works, Inc.

Torah

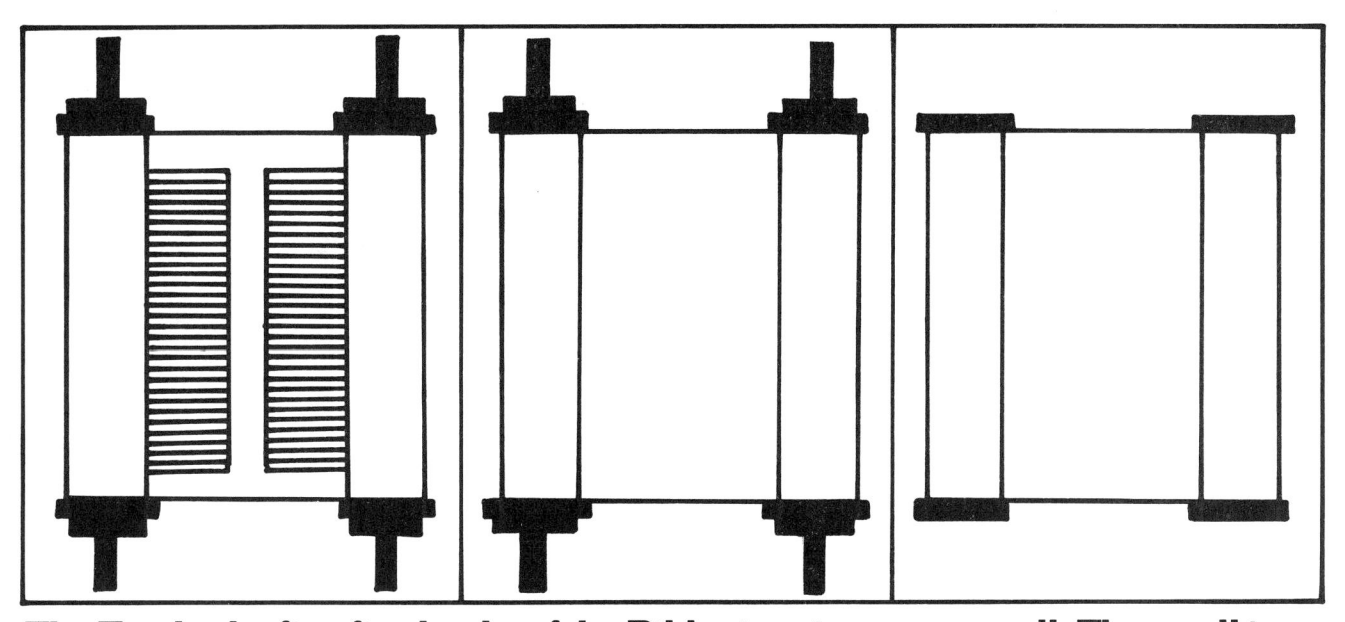

The Torah, the first five books of the Bible, is written on a scroll. The scroll is on two wooden rollers. Each roller is called an *etz hayim,* which means "tree of life." Draw someone reading the Torah.

JEWISH SUPERDOODLES
© The Learning Works, Inc.

yad

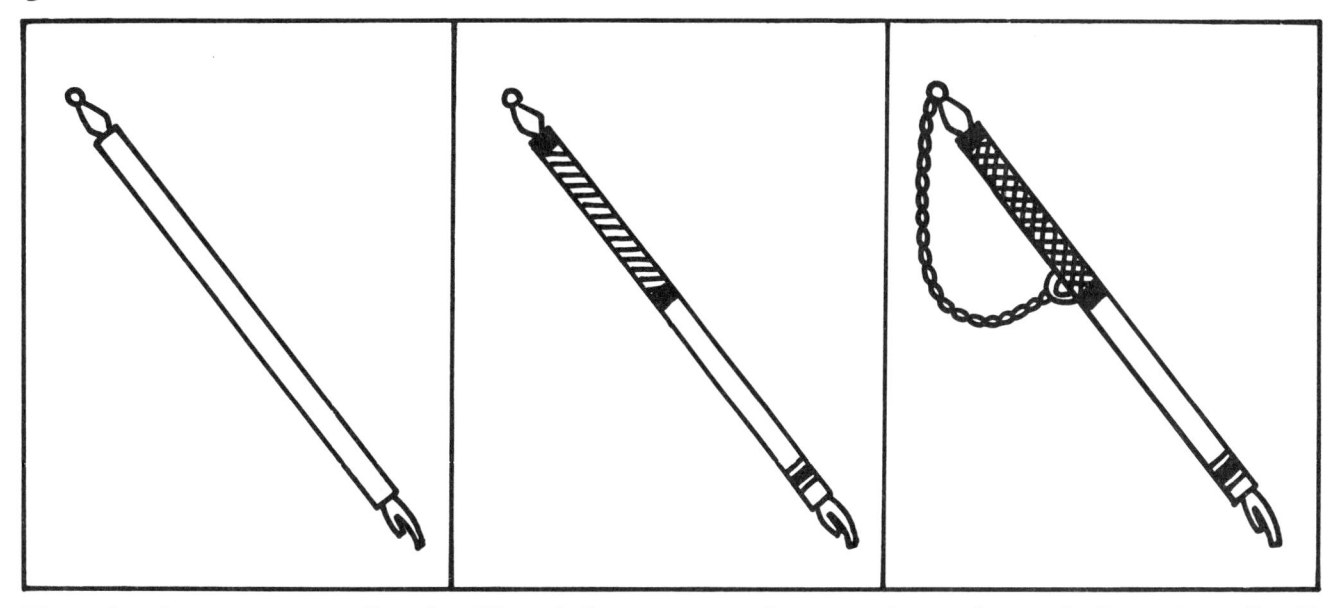

People show respect for the Torah by not touching it directly with their hands. A *yad* is a special pointer used when reading the Torah. Yad is the Hebrew word for "hand." Draw someone holding a yad and reading from the Torah.

JECC/RMC
012471